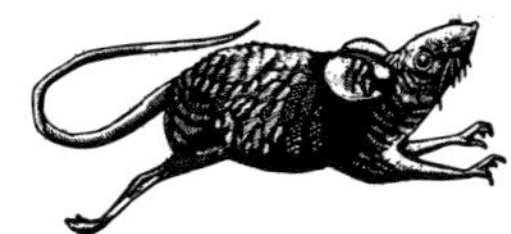

McCurdy's World

Prints and Drawings by Michael McCurdy

A Postcard Book by Michael McCurdy

Capra Press
Santa Barbara

Printed in the United States of America.

ISBN 0-88496-354-3

CAPRA PRESS
Post Office Box 2068
Santa Barbara, California 93120

Burins, Blocks and Books

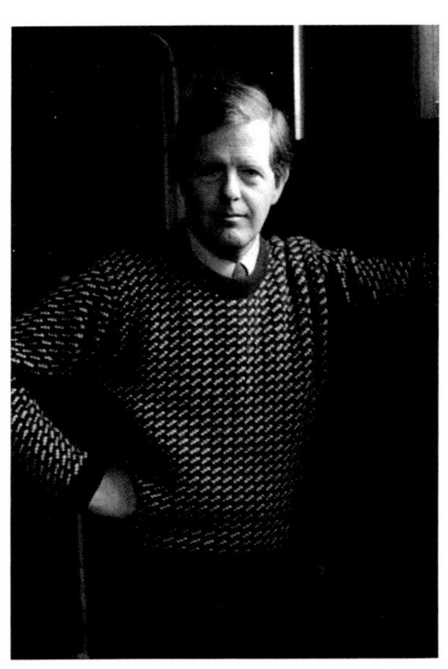

Most of these pictures are wood engravings, images created by cutting laboriously into end-grain wood blocks of polished maple, using pointed tools with wooden handles called burins. The black areas in these prints are the raised parts on the wood block that were left untouched. The white areas are those that were cut away so not to print when the paper was impressed upon the inked wood block.

Some of the images in this collection were done in scratchboard, known in England as "scraperboard." The process is similar to wood engraving—it requires the same kind of thinking in reverse, though it saves a great deal of elbow grease. A special tool is scratched along on the inked clay-surfaced board to remove black areas, just as a burin whittles away little curlicues of wood from the block. A major difference is that scratchboard is really a drawing. A finished image is produced directly, rather than an incised engraving which then needs to be printed to be seen.

The year of this postcard book's publication happens to be the thirtieth anniversary of my first wood engraving. The process sneaked into my psyche and doesn't let go. Wood engravers certainly are their own breed. Why does this inclination to cut away images from darkened surfaces of inch-high wood blocks persist? It's just the opposite of what most artists like to do. They seem to prefer lighter and more colorful creations. Nevertheless, nothing quite sings like black and white. Its graphic power can carry the day. Blacks, whites and grays transmit their own special kind of color.

It's been noted that many wood engravers dwell in colder climates, and that perhaps this black-art approach is somehow related to people who harbor a stubborn streak born of bitter winters in unheated rooms. Perhaps the climate and hilly enclaves of New England encourage introspective types who actually enjoy sitting hunched over a magnifying glass and conjuring up little worlds on their blackened blocks. Even so, engraving has integrity and leaves no margin for error. It's not big and splashy. It simply grabbed me and wouldn't let go.

I am a book artist, first and foremost. I made these pictures for adult trade books, children's books, and rare limited edition books. Though they have their origins in images, they also grew from my own world. Images can be windows and doors that bid one welcome. These pictures were done as much for you, the reader and viewer, as for me. I hope you enjoy them.

~ MICHAEL McCURDY

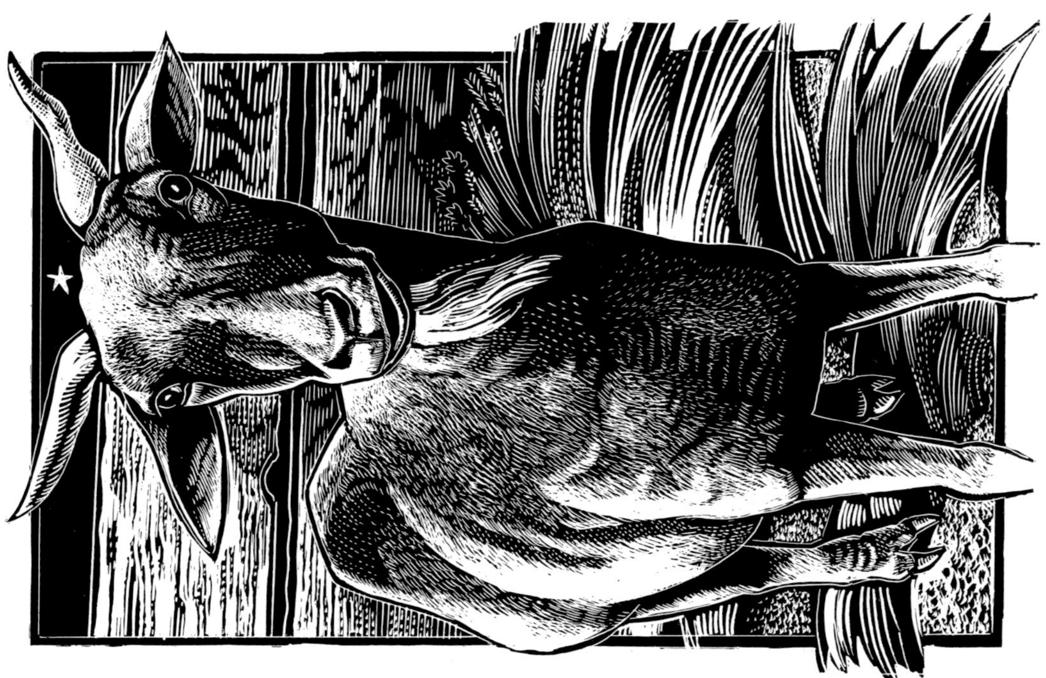

GOAT from *McCurdy's World*

Copyright © 1992 by Michael McCurdy

CAPRA PRESS   SANTA BARBARA

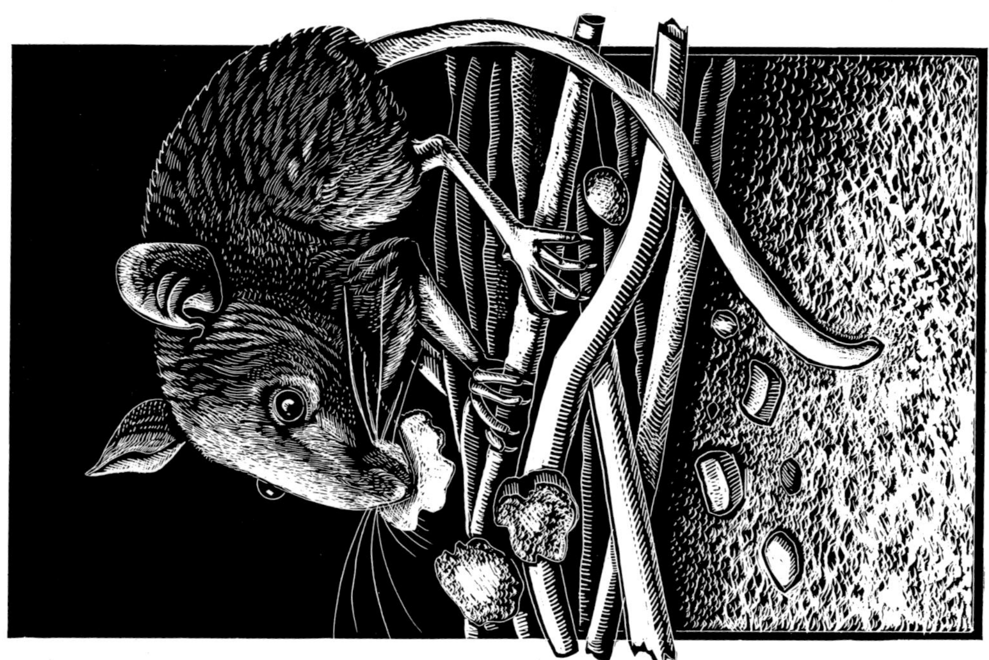

Mouse from *McCurdy's World*

Copyright © 1992 by Michael McCurdy

CAPRA PRESS   SANTA BARBARA

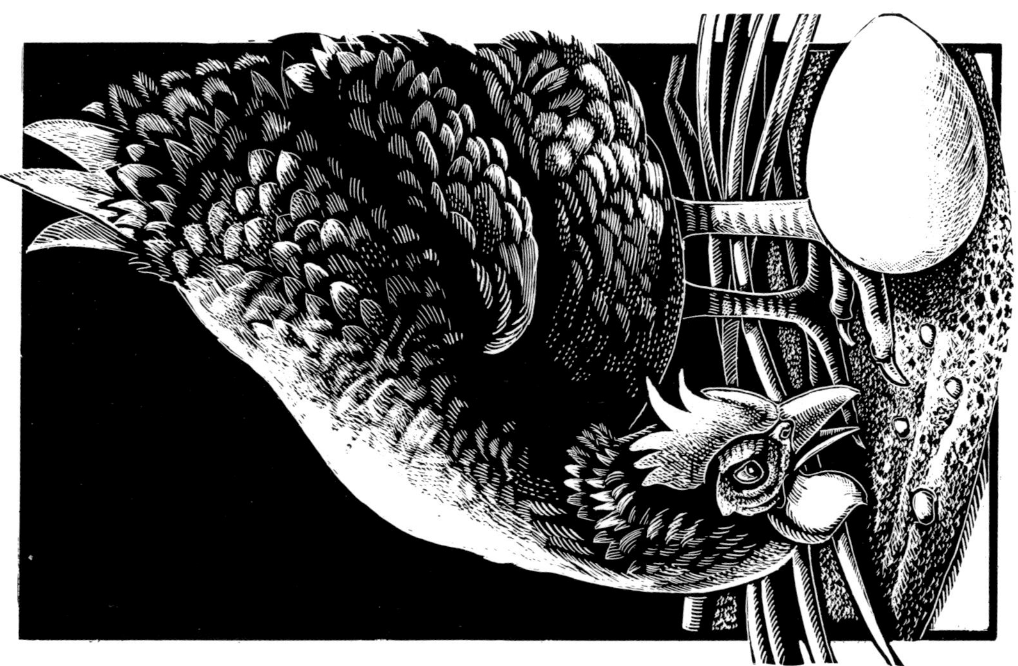

Chicken from *McCurdy's World*

Copyright © 1992 by Michael McCurdy

CAPRA PRESS   SANTA BARBARA

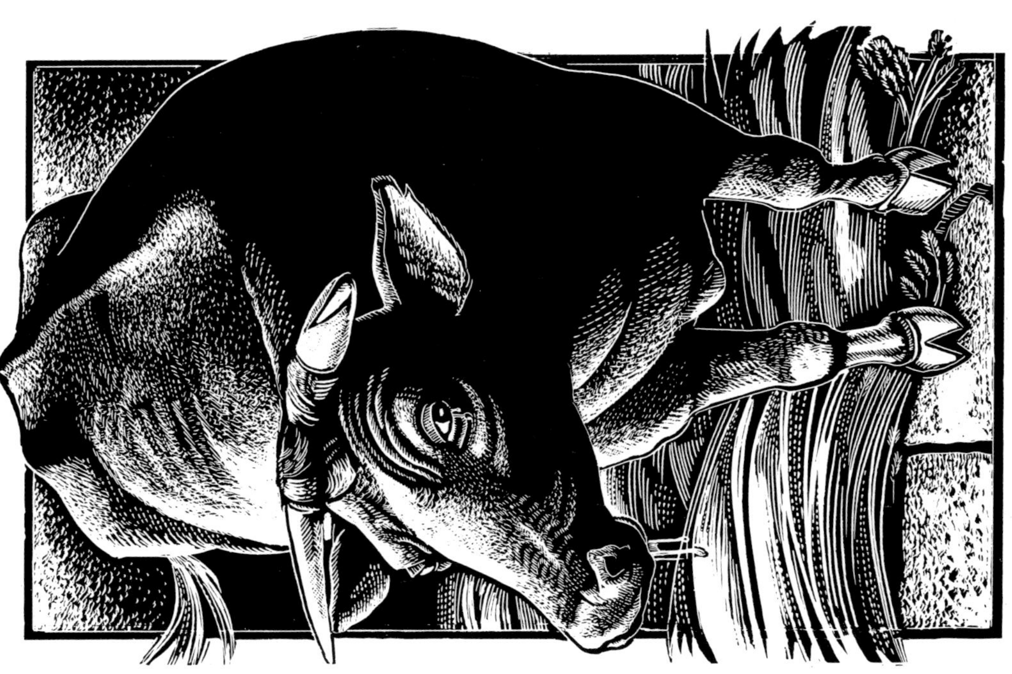

Ox from *McCurdy's World*

Copyright © 1992 by Michael McCurdy

CAPRA PRESS   SANTA BARBARA

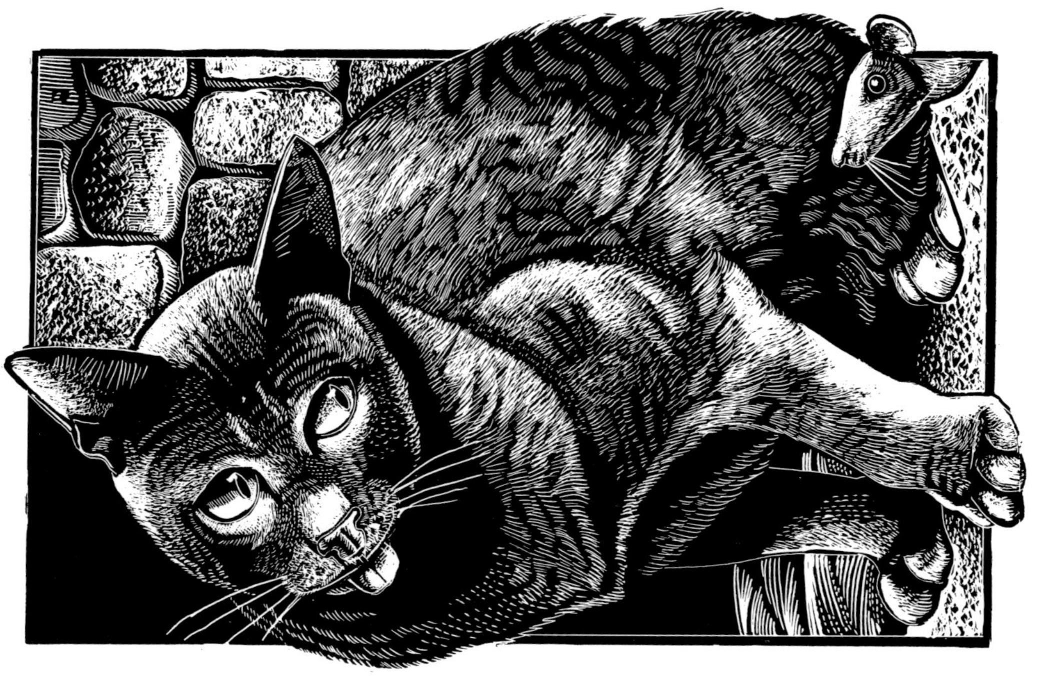

Cᴀᴛ from *McCurdy's World*

Copyright © 1992 by Michael McCurdy

Cᴀᴘʀᴀ Pʀᴇss   Sᴀɴᴛᴀ Bᴀʀʙᴀʀᴀ

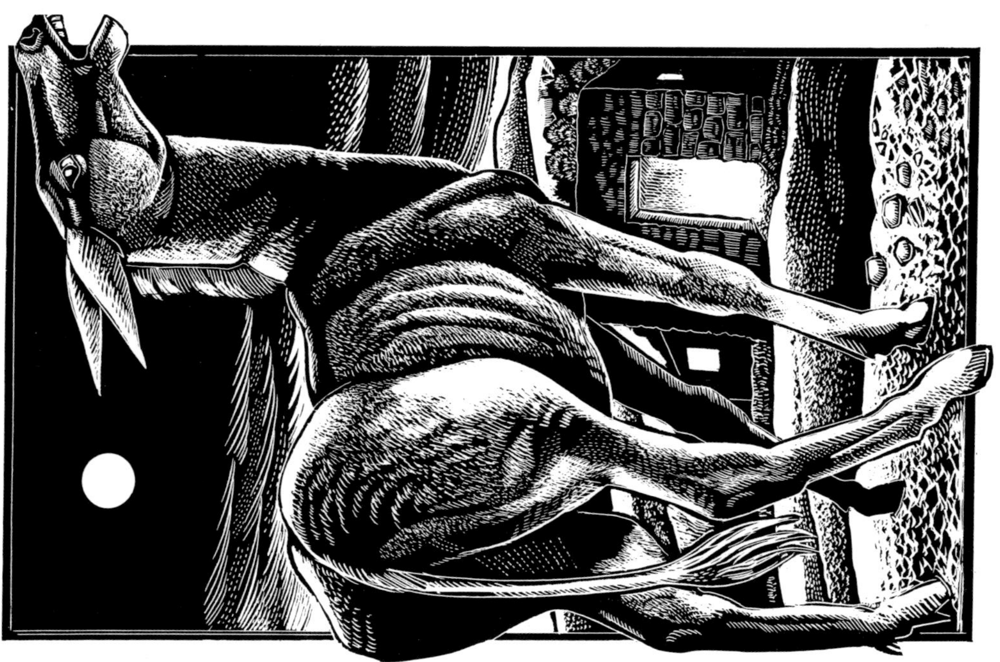

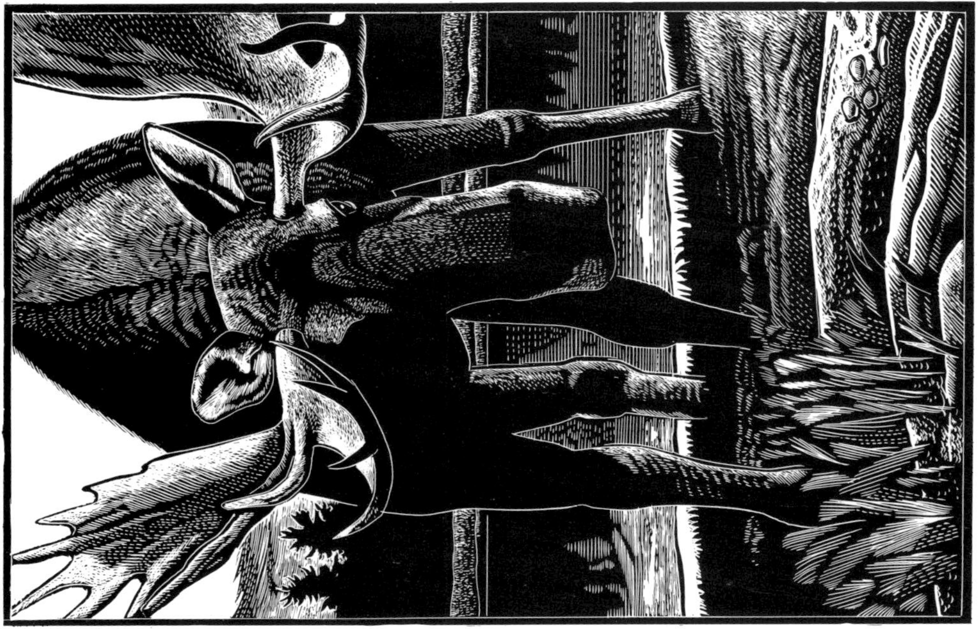

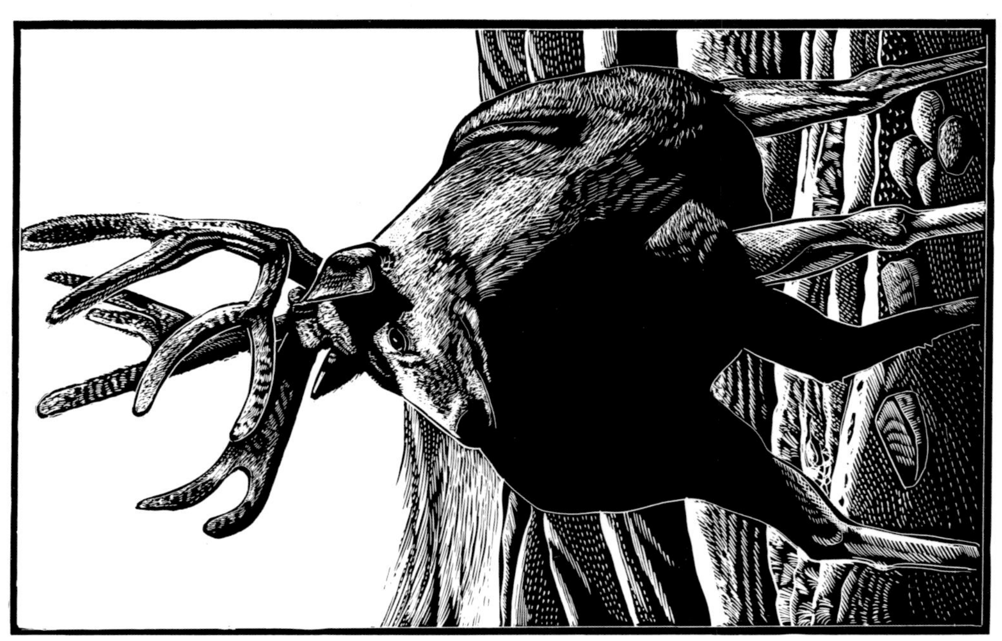

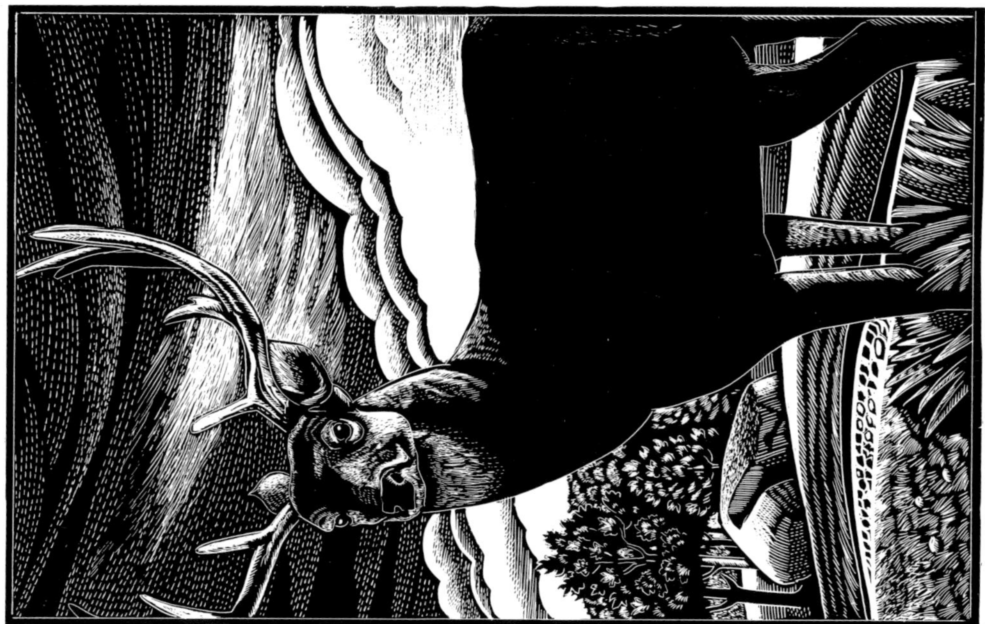

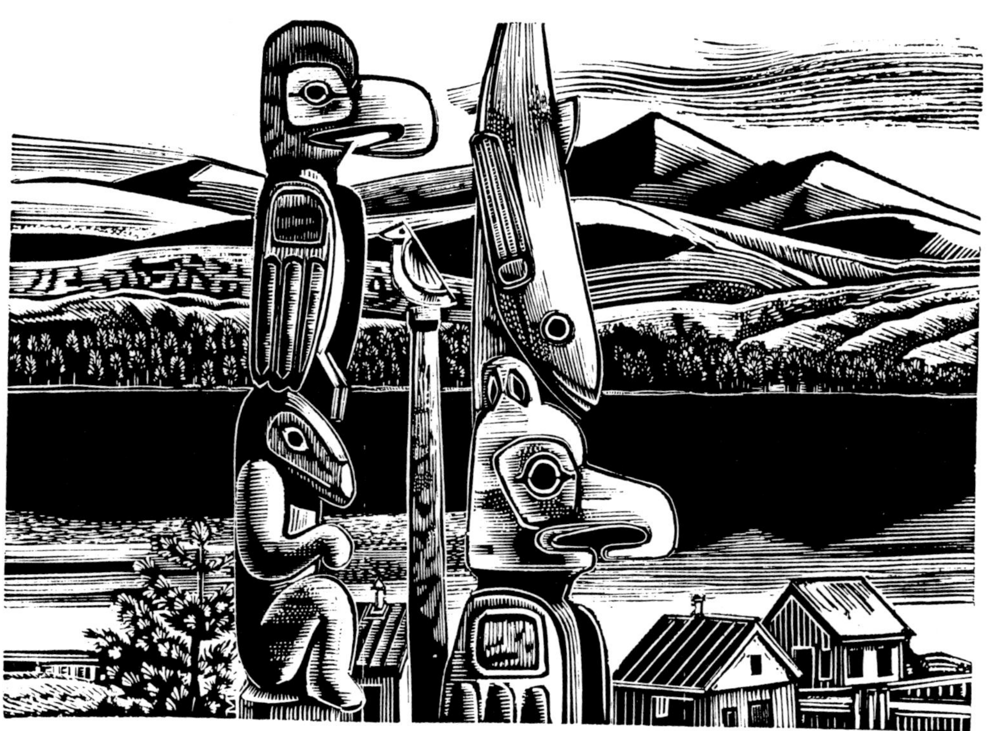

CAPRA PRESS   SANTA BARBARA

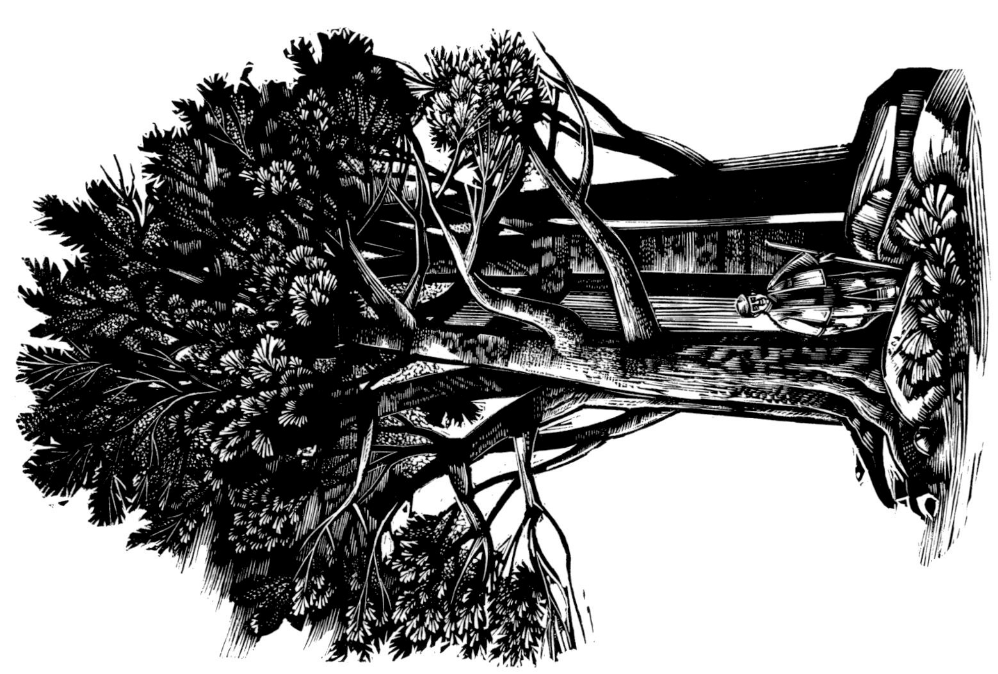

MAN AND TREES from *McCurdy's World*

Copyright © 1992 by Michael McCurdy

CAPRA PRESS   SANTA BARBARA

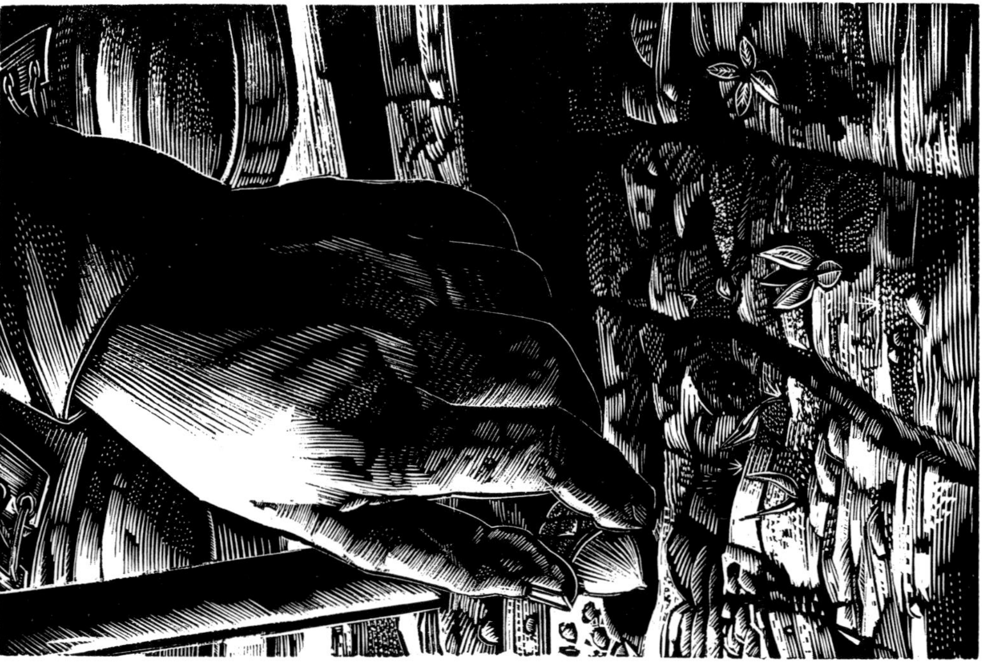

CAPRA PRESS   SANTA BARBARA

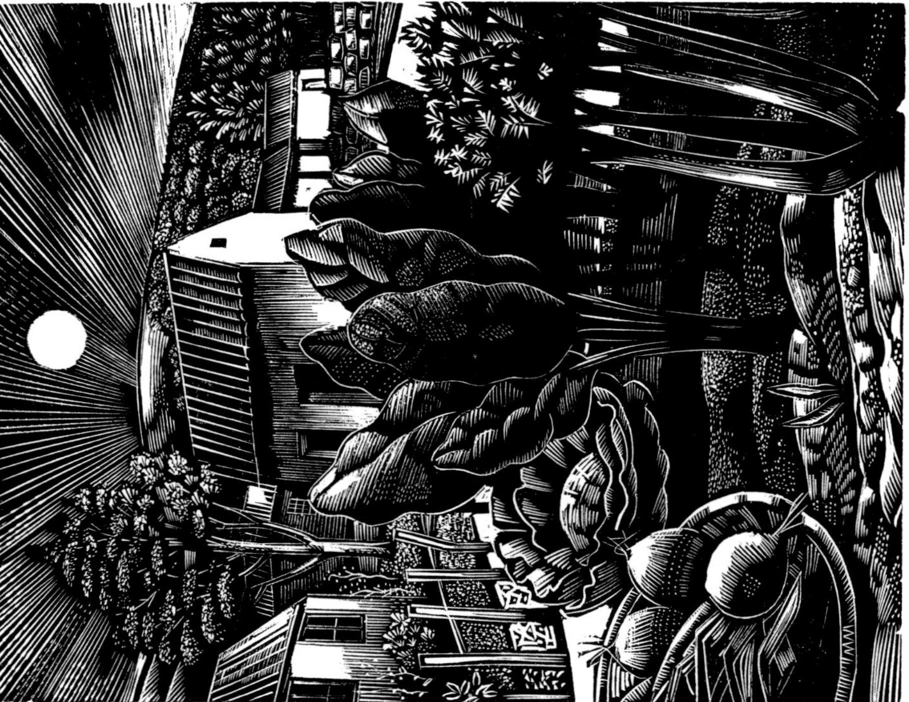

Garden from *McCurdy's World*

Copyright © 1992 by Michael McCurdy

CAPRA PRESS   SANTA BARBARA

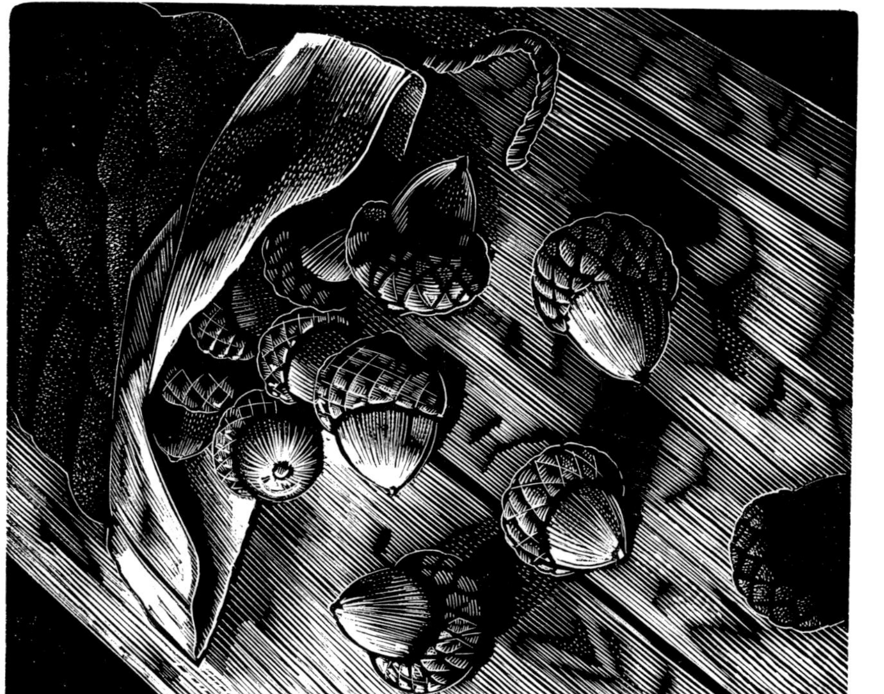

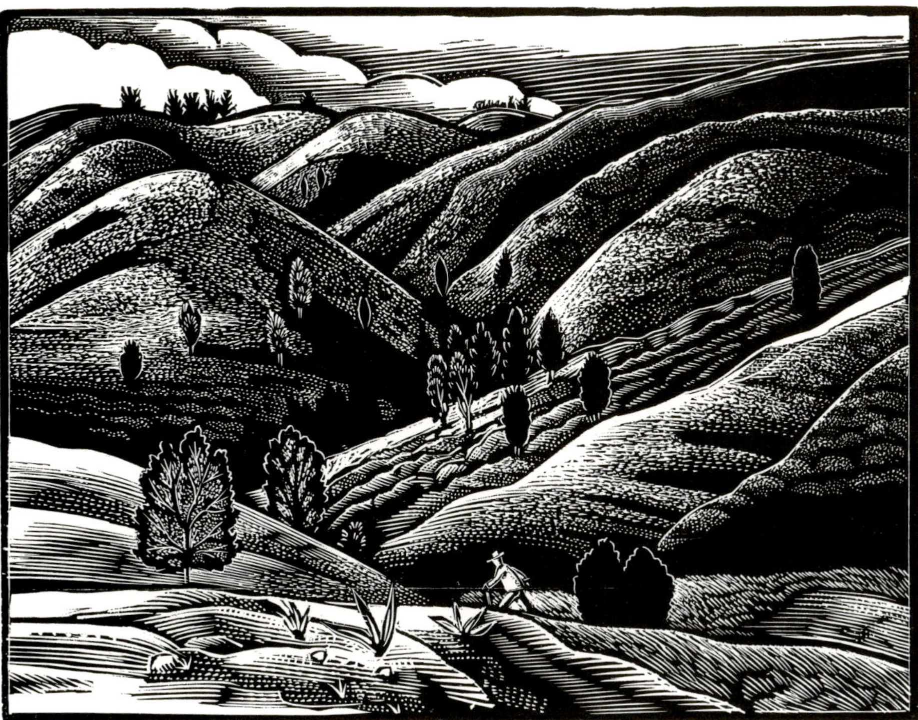

Sᴍᴇʀʀᴀ Fᴏᴏᴛʜɪʟʟs **from** *McCurdy's World*

Copyright © 1992 by Michael McCurdy

CAPRA PRESS   SANTA BARBARA

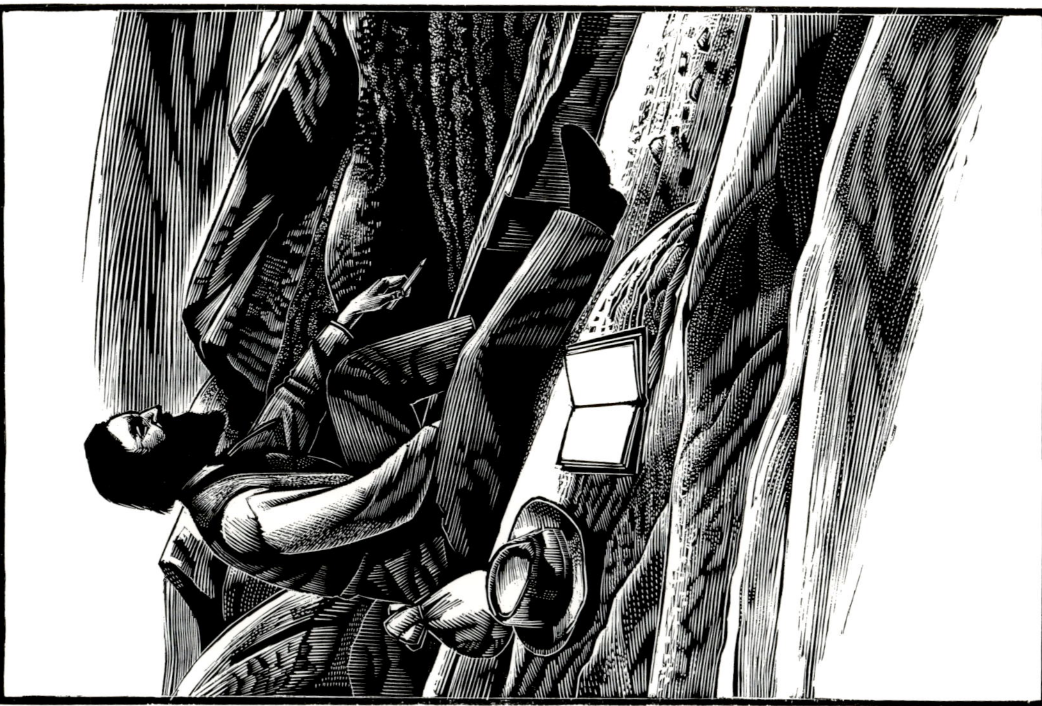

John Muir on North Dome from *McCurdy's World*

Copyright © 1992 by Michael McCurdy

CAPRA PRESS　SANTA BARBARA

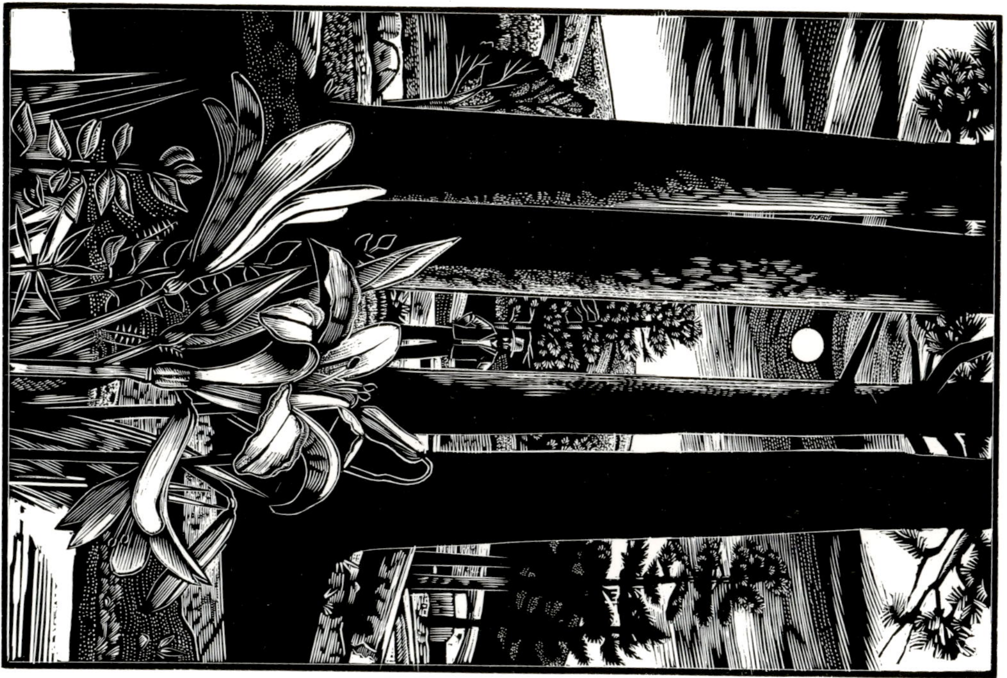

Washington Lillies, Sierra from *McCurdy's World*

Copyright © 1992 by Michael McCurdy

CAPRA PRESS   SANTA BARBARA

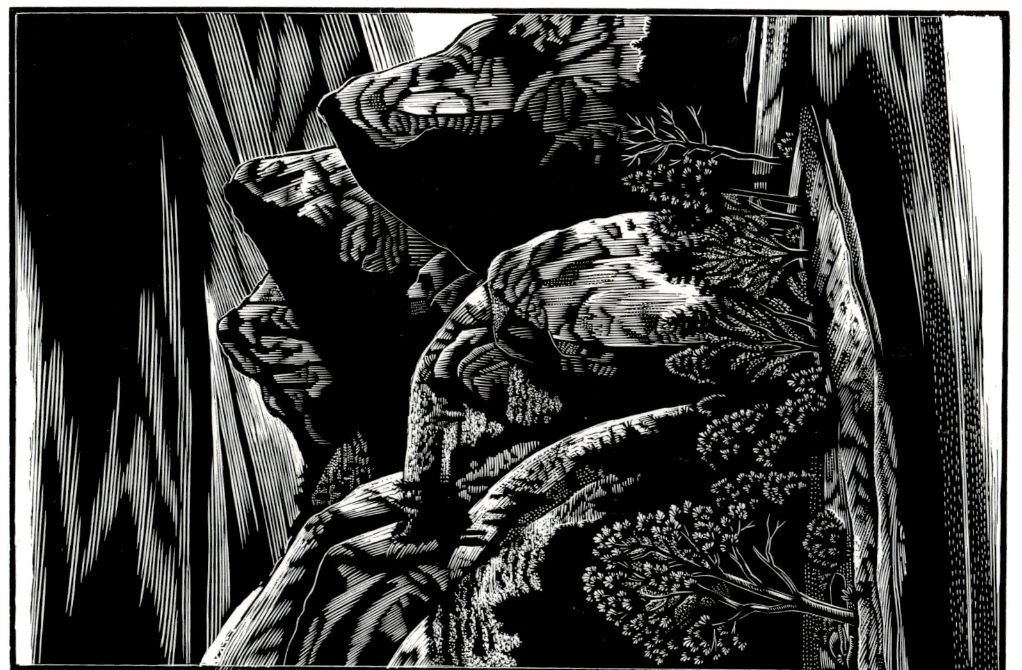

Three Brothers, Yosemite **from** *McCurdy's World*

Copyright © 1992 by Michael McCurdy

CAPRA PRESS   SANTA BARBARA

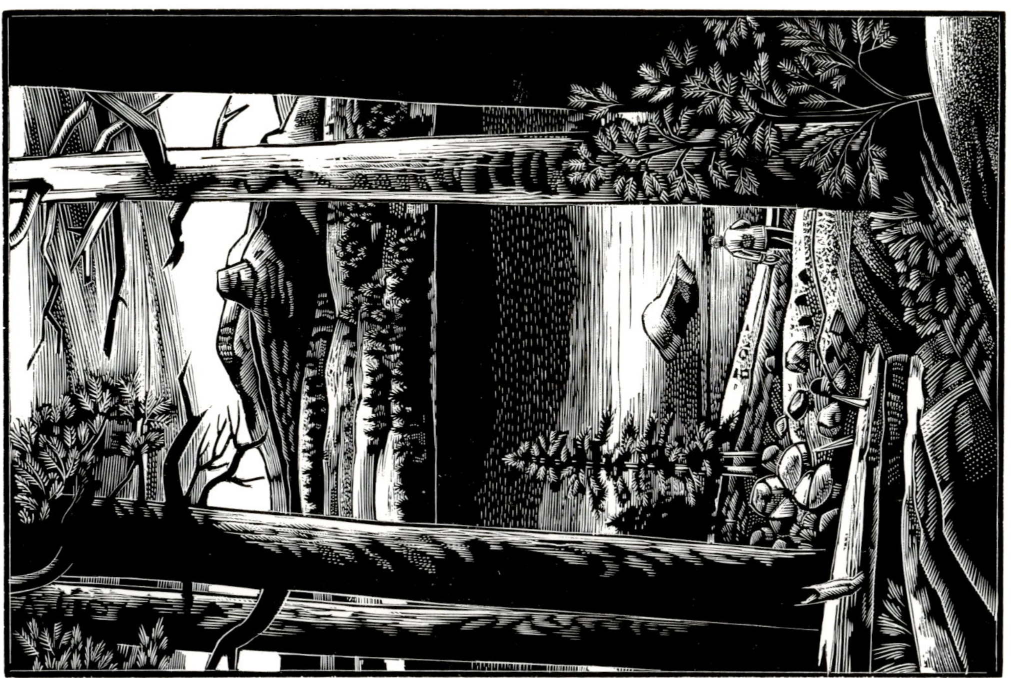

Lᴀᴋᴇ Tᴇɴᴀʏᴀ, Sɪᴇʀʀᴀ **from** *McCurdy's World*

Copyright © 1992 by Michael McCurdy

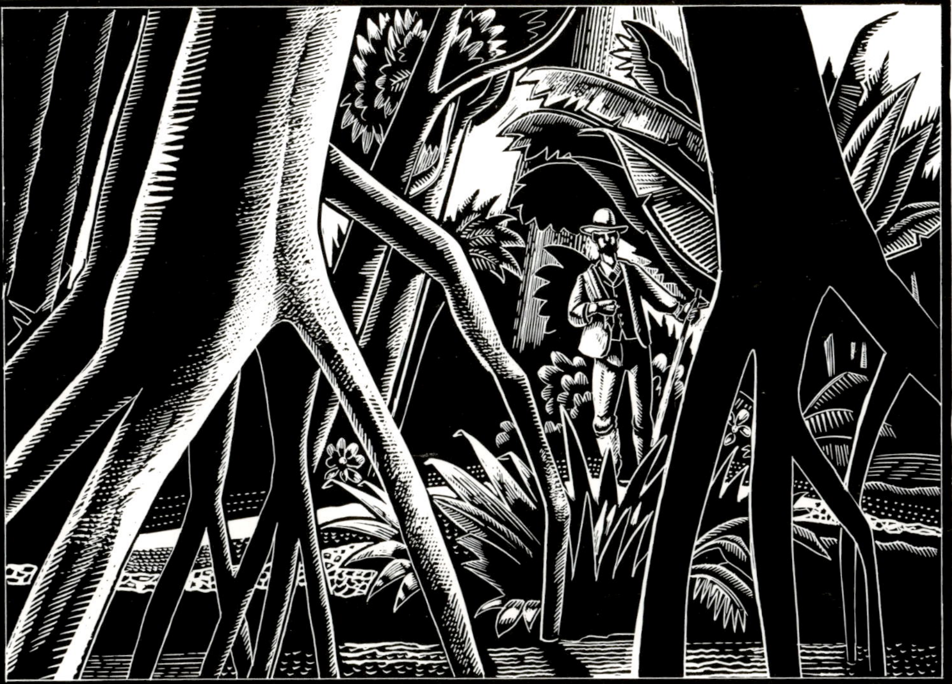

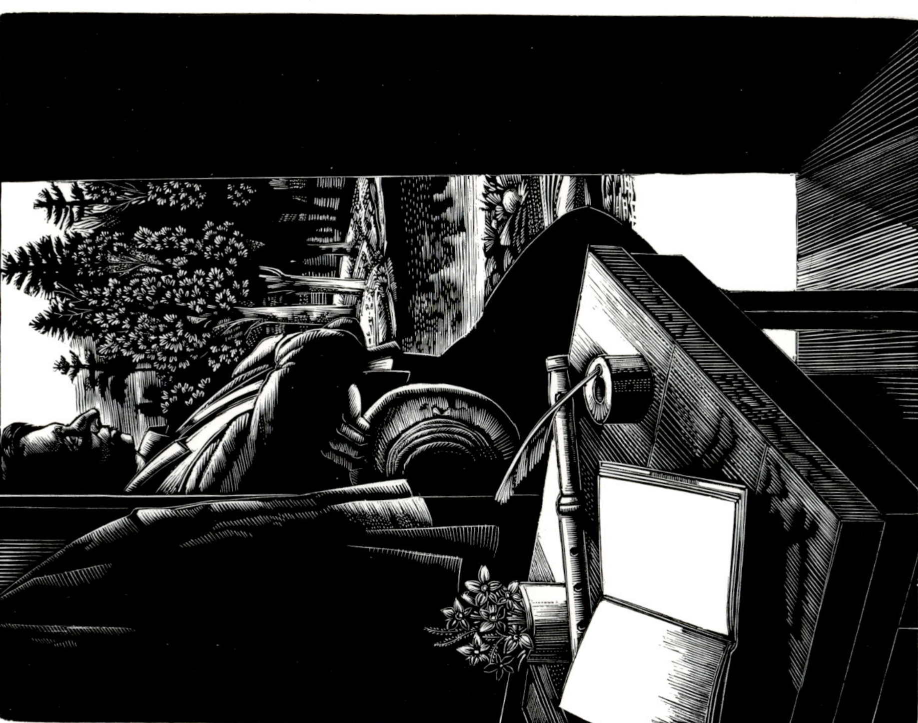

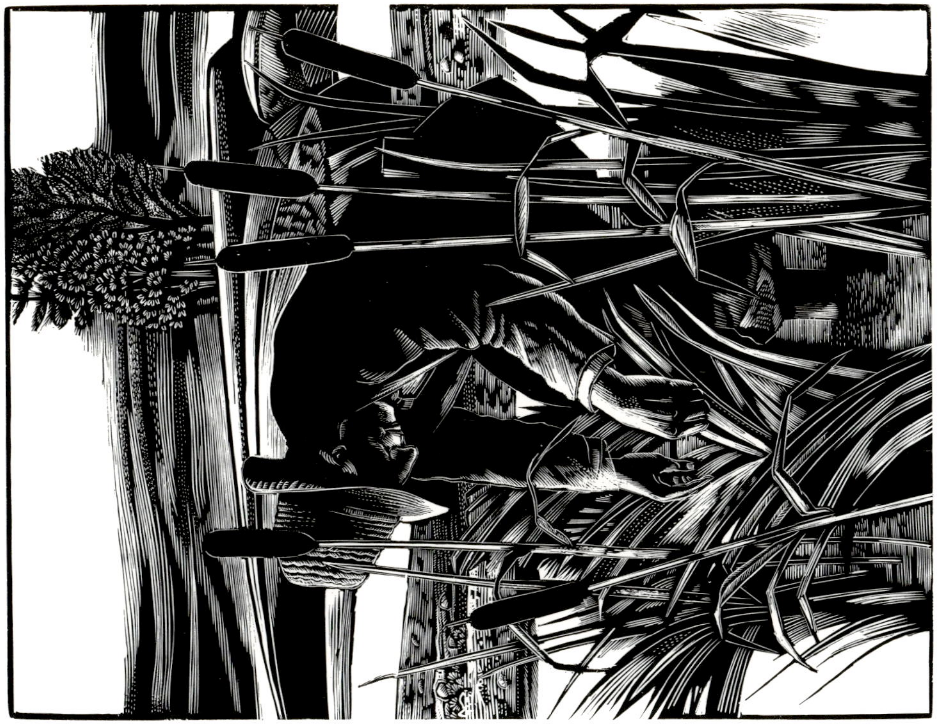

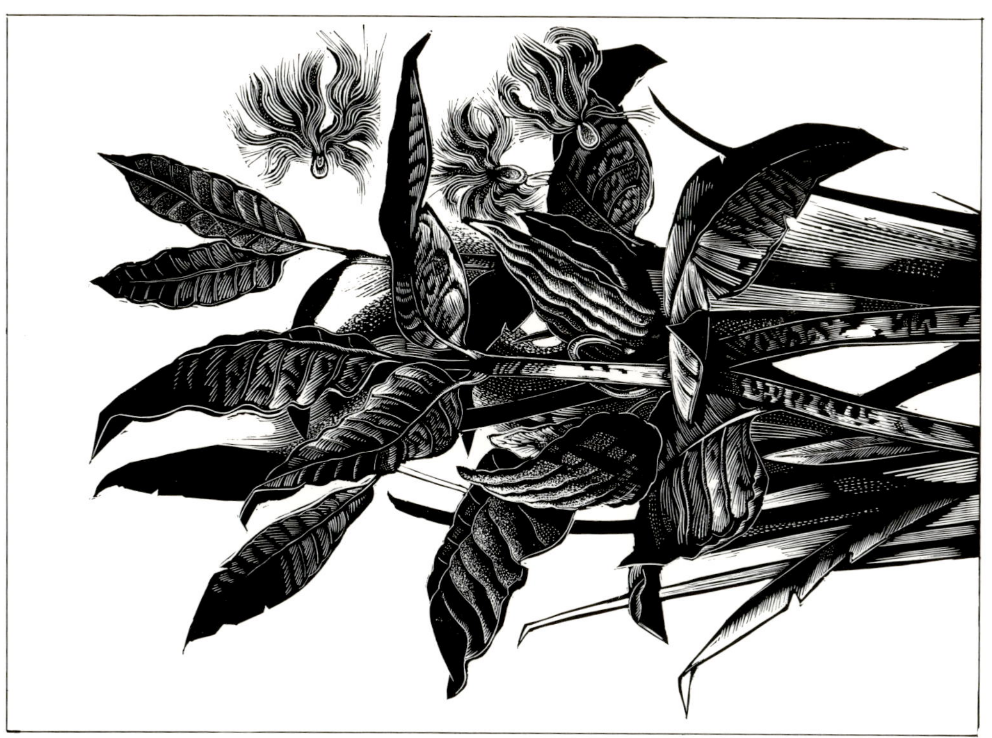

CAPRA PRESS   SANTA BARBARA

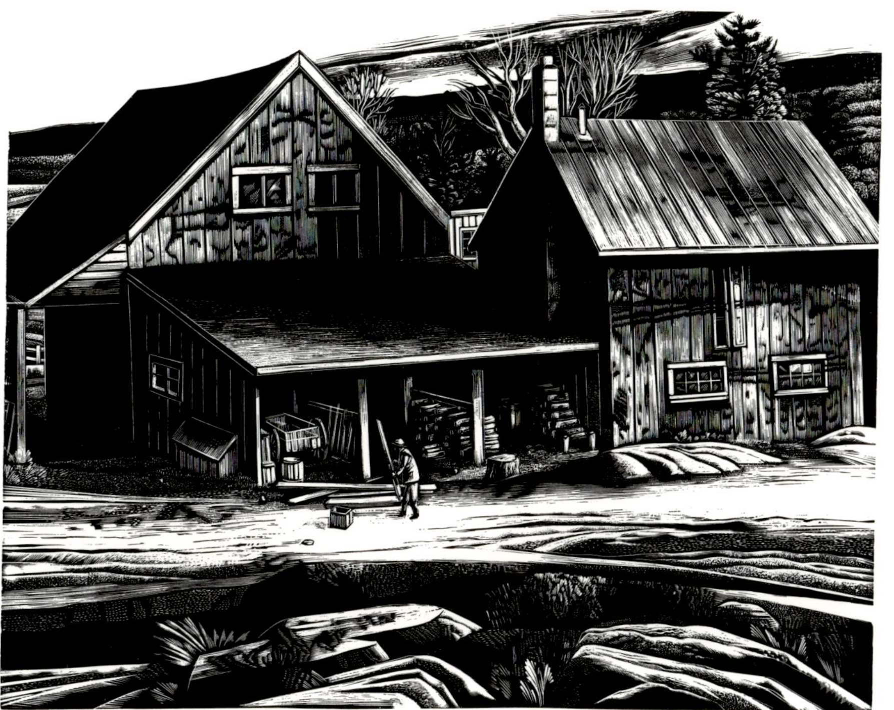

Last Snow from *McCurdy's World*

Copyright © 1992 by Michael McCurdy

CAPRA PRESS   SANTA BARBARA

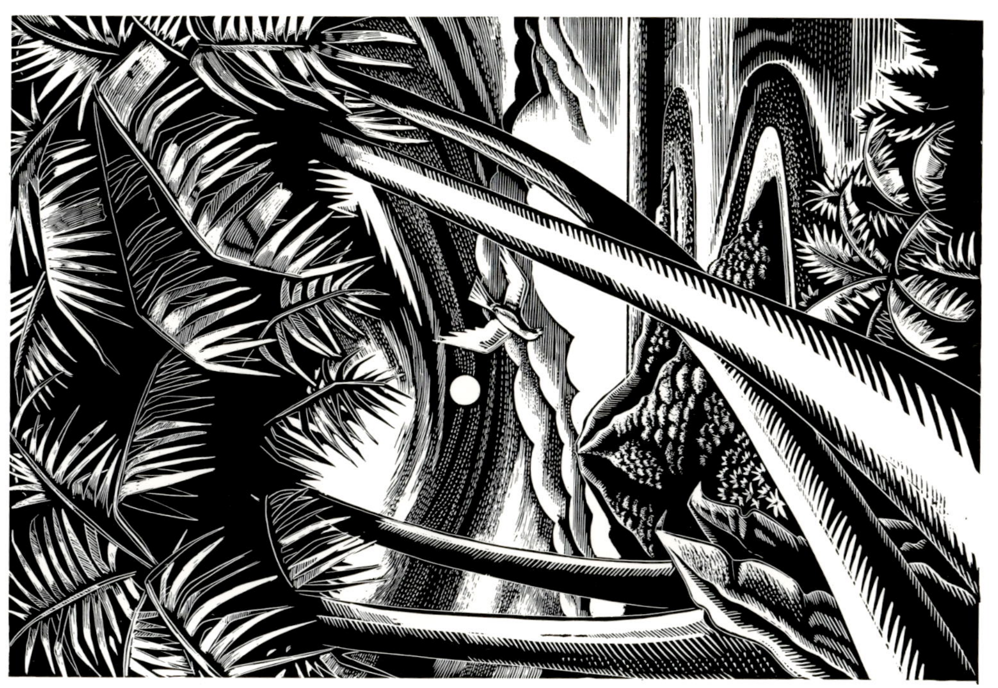

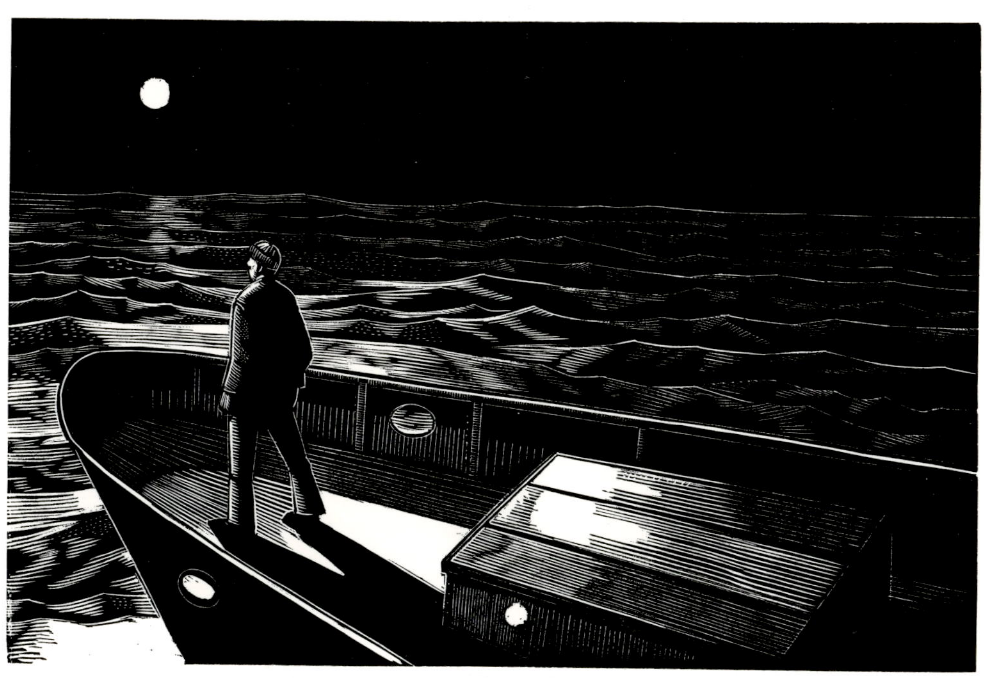

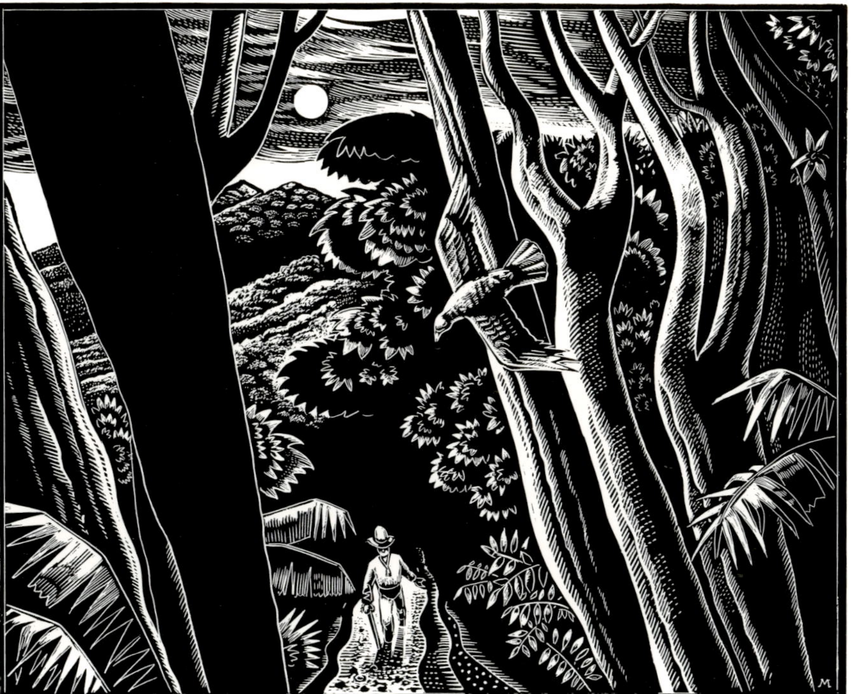

Jungle Trek from *McCurdy's World*

Copyright © 1992 by Michael McCurdy

CAPRA PRESS SANTA BARBARA

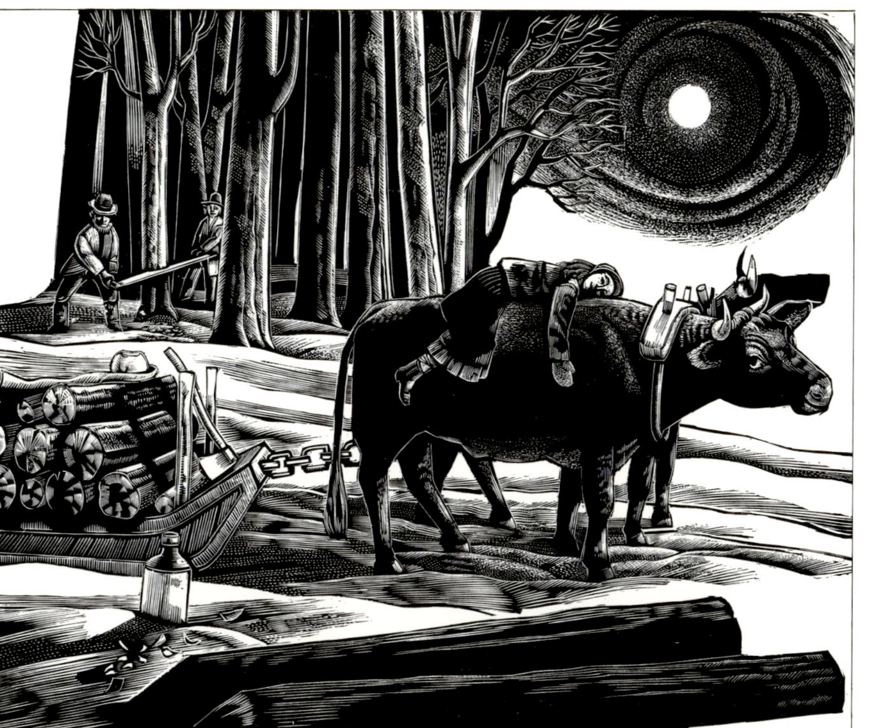

Hannah and the Ox from *McCurdy's World*

Copyright © 1992 by Michael McCurdy

CAPRA PRESS   SANTA BARBARA

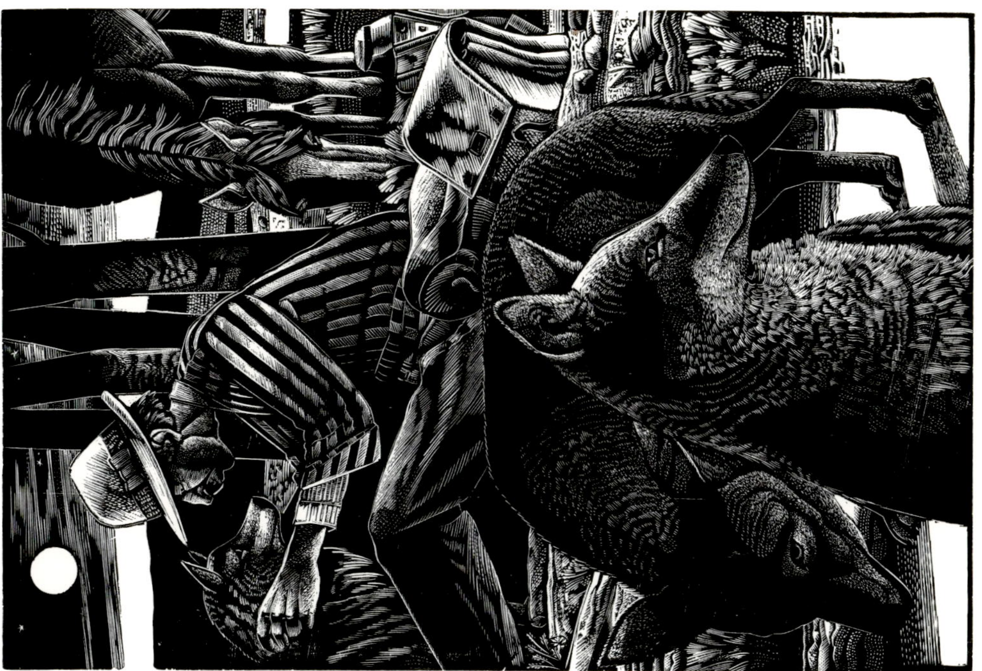

SEVEN RIVERS WEST from *McCurdy's World*

Copyright © 1992 by Michael McCurdy

CAPRA PRESS SANTA BARBARA

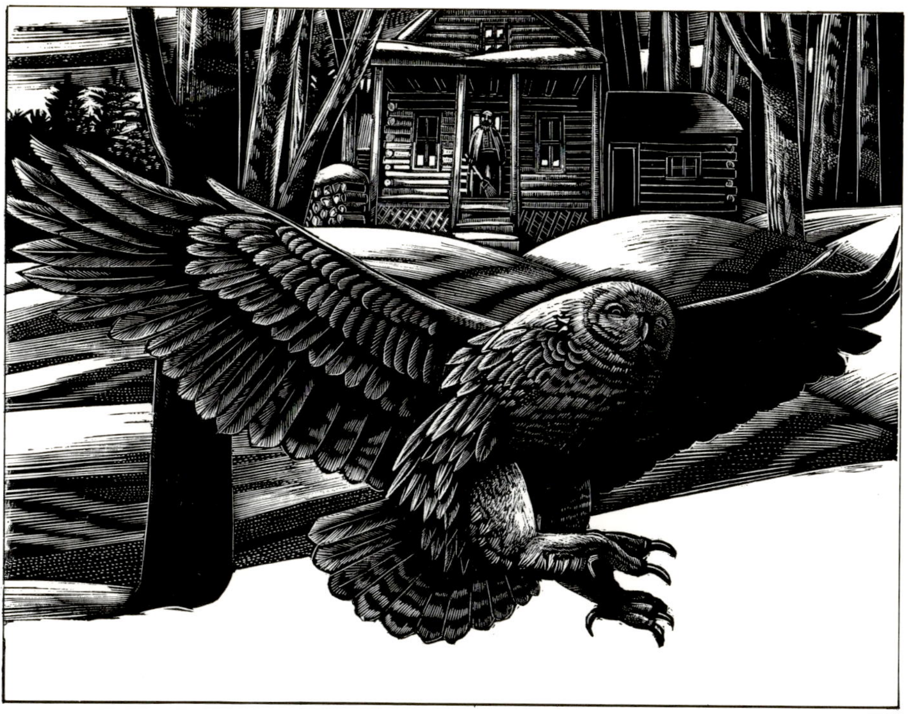

OWL-SCATTERER from *McCurdy's World*
Copyright © 1992 by Michael McCurdy

CAPRA PRESS • SANTA BARBARA